Linking art to the world around us

artyfacts
Communication

Contents

WRITTEN BY John Stringer

Rows of beads

Imagine you are in Ancient Egypt. An old merchant approaches his first customer of the day. The merchant has made a long journey to sell perfumes and other luxury goods and is sure of making a good profit. As the sale progresses, he pulls out an object that consists of rows of wooden rods threaded with beads. As he calculates prices, he flicks the beads across the rows at great speed. He counts faster than if he were using a modern calculator! The instrument he is using is an abacus – the ancestor of our modern computer.

INTERNATIONAL COMPUTER

The abacus, a simple counting tool and the first 'computer', was invented by people in many different parts of the world. The Ancient Egyptians and the Babylonians were using it 5,000 years ago, as were the Chinese. When the Spanish first reached America in the 1500s, they found the Mayan people using it too.

SPEED COUNT

The beads in each row represent numbers. In a base-ten abacus, there would be a ones rod, a tens rod, a hundreds rod, and so on. The beads are pushed along the rows to build totals.

Counting frame

WHAT YOU NEED

shoebox

air-drying clay

string

glitter

paints and brush

knitting needle

1 Decorate your box with coloured paint. Use the knitting needle to poke three holes, one above the other, in each side of the box as shown.

2 Roll 30 pieces of clay into small round balls and push the knitting needle through the middle of each to make a hole. Leave to dry.

3 Decorate the balls with paints and glitter.

Use your abacus to count single units on the bottom row, tens on the middle row, and hundreds on the top one.

4

Thread three lengths of string through the holes on one side of the box, and secure with a knot. Thread 10 balls onto each piece.

5

Push the other end of the string through the second hole. Pull tightly and tie firmly.

Use your abacus to make high-speed calculations!

5

Flying flags

A flag is usually a piece of cloth with a special design on it. A flag can stand for a person, a country, an organisation, or it can give information. All nations, and many states, towns and cities, have their own flags. So do organisations like the Scouts or the Red Cross. Flags may also be used to send messages.

FIRST FLAGS

In Ancient Egypt, flag-like objects appeared in wall paintings. These 'flags' consisted of symbols attached to the tops of poles. The first cloth flags were used in China around 3000 BC and were made of silk. In Europe in the Middle Ages, soldiers called knights carried a square flag with a streamer.

A knight who was promoted to a higher position had this flag cut off and replaced with a new flag called a banner. These high-ranking knights were called 'bannerets'.

FLAG COLOURS

There are seven basic colours generally used in national flags: red, white, green, orange, black, yellow and blue.

FLAGS AT SEA

Flags were used at sea before the days of radio communication to send messages to other ships or to shore. There was a complex system of designs for these flags. One ship would salute another by dipping its flags. These salutes played a major part in international diplomacy at sea.

6

Bright banners

WHAT
YOU
NEED

coloured
paper

scissors

string

glue

white
paper

paints

pencil

paintbrush

String up your flags to brighten up a party or special occasion

1 Cut triangular and square shapes out of coloured and patterned paper.

2 Fold the shapes over on one side and glue them to a length of string.

3 On white paper, draw and paint some simple pictures to fit on the flags.

4 Cut out the pictures, glue them onto the flags and hang them up.

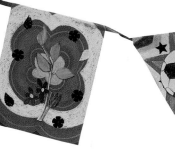

Knots for counting

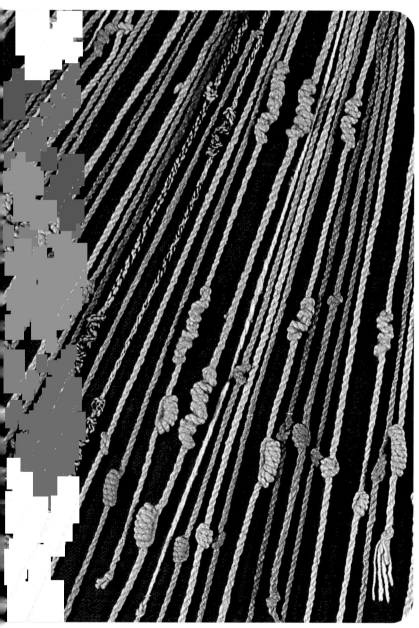

MEASURING WITH STRING
The Inca people of South America tied knots in strings of different lengths and colours. The knots were used for counting and for keeping records of sums and figures. The Incas called these knotted strings 'quipus'. Each colour or knot in a quipu meant something different. The knots could also be of different sizes and spaced at different intervals to represent numbers.

LOG CHIP AND LINE
Knots were once used on ships to measure how fast they were travelling. Every ship carried a measuring device called a log chip and line. The line was wound around a reel while the chip, a piece of wood, was dragged in the water behind the ship. As the ship moved along, this made the line unwind.

HOW MANY KNOTS?
The line had knots tied in it at regular intervals of 14.4 metres. At the end of the first interval was one knot, at the end of the second were two knots, and so on. The line was allowed to run for 28 seconds (28 seconds was the same proportion of an hour, as 14.4 metres was of a nautical mile). So if the log line had run out to five intervals in 28 seconds, the sailors knew the ship was moving at a speed of 5 'knots', or 5 nautical miles per hour.

MISSISSIPPI MARKS
Mississippi paddle steamers used lines with knots in them to measure the depth of the river, as it could get dangerously shallow. Each knot was called a 'mark'. A depth of two knots, called a 'mark twain', was 3.7 metres, a safe depth for the boats.

Knots are used for tying up many different things, including shoes, boxes and boats. But knots can have other uses too. They can even be used for counting!

Quipu Curtain

You could hang this on your wall, in a doorway or in a window

string

scissors

beads

bamboo stick

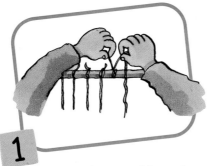

1 Cut eight equal lengths of string and tie to the bamboo stick.

2 Knot together each pair of strings, moving along the row. Then repeat, knotting alternate strings together.

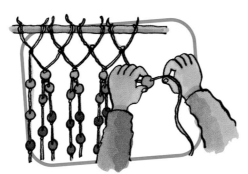

3 Thread a bead onto each length of string, and tie a knot to hold it on. Add as many beads and knots as you like to all the strings.

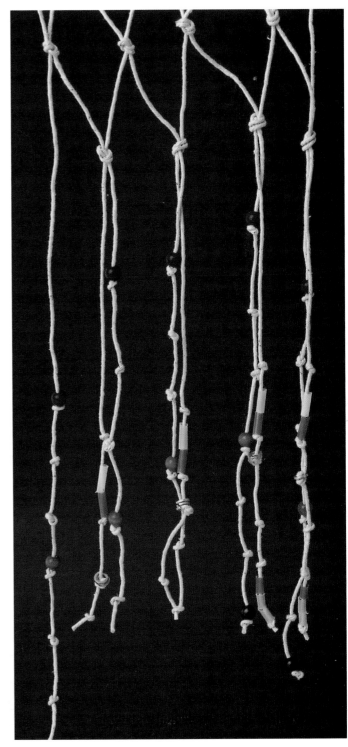

9

Signs and symbols

Before alphabets and writing were invented, many people told stories, sent messages or kept lists using symbols and pictures. Ancient Egyptian writing used pictures instead of words. Each picture, called a hieroglyph, was a sign that stood for a name, a place, an object or a meaning. Hieroglyphs took a long time to write. And with no full stops, commas and sentences, it is hard to tell where to start reading and where to stop!

SCRATCHES ON CLAY

The first people to write lived in Sumer (part of the modern country of Iraq) 10,000 years ago. They scratched simple pictures on clay tablets to help them remember details about their land, animals and crops.

SOUNDS SYSTEM

The biggest step in the story of writing was to have symbols that stood for spoken sounds instead of for objects or ideas. This made writing easier, because the scribes – the writers – only had to learn the symbol for each sound. This style of writing was copied by many nations. And over time, the symbols slowly changed into alphabets.

Ancient Egyptian hieroglyphs (above). The famous Rosetta stone, which has ancient hieroglyphs scratched on it (below).

Calligraphic art

WHAT YOU NEED

teabags

strong white paper

fine paintbrush

black paint

paints and brush

pencil

coloured card

1 Brush cold black tea on both sides of the paper with a paintbrush. Allow the paper to dry.

2 Draw imaginary Japanese, Chinese, or Arabic characters in pencil.

3 Paint over the characters with watery black paint.

4 Finish the painting with an imaginary red seal and signature.

5 Mount on coloured card.

Design your own symbol or character alphabet and write secret messages to your friends

11

Smoke and drums

Before telephone and e-mail, people had to send information over long distances by much simpler methods. Sometimes this involved sending signals that could be interpreted as words or ideas. Two of the earliest ways to send signals were by beating a drum and by creating puffs of smoke. Drums can be heard over long distances, and smoke can be seen from far away.

DRUM MESSAGES

The first drums were probably made of animal skin stretched over a hollow log. The booming noise they made when they were beaten could be used to send a message quickly over a long distance. Only simple messages, such as a warning, could be sent. Drum signals were used by Native Americans in the USA and by many African and Asian peoples.

PUFFS OF SMOKE

Smoke signals can be made by lighting a fire made with green wood which makes plenty of smoke. The Native Americans held blankets over the fire to hold down the smoke, then let it rise into the sky in a special way. The number of puffs, or the delay between puffs, could be 'read' by members of the tribe. Smoke signals were an effective way of signalling danger: for instance, warning that a troop of soliders was coming. Signals might also be used to tell others about good hunting – perhaps sending details about a herd of buffalo.

Talking drum

Make and decorate a drum and bang out all kinds of secret messages!

WHAT YOU NEED

plastic container with lid

tissue paper

glitter or sequins

glue

paints and paintbrush

1 Glue strips of coloured tissue paper onto your container so that it is covered all over.

2 Decorate it with sequins, beads, buttons or any other materials.

You can invent a special signals code!

3 Paint the lid a bright colour and leave to dry.

Shake, rattle and bang!

Make different sounds by putting pebbles or sand inside the container. Now you can shake your drum as well.

13

Codes and ciphers

Secret messages are usually sent in code. A code, or cipher, is a made-up language. It can be a series of words, letters, numbers, pictures or symbols, which you use instead of normal language. For example, you can replace each letter of the alphabet with the next. So, a message saying: "IFSF JT B TFDSFU" means "Here is a secret".

CAESAR'S CODE

Codes can be useful for keeping information from an enemy. The Roman leader, Julius Caesar, was one of the first code makers. He replaced each letter with one three places along in the alphabet. To read this code, a cipher disc was used. It had two turning discs printed with letters and numbers. The outer disc was turned to line up a letter in the message with a letter on the inner disc. Each letter of the message would then be replaced by a code letter.

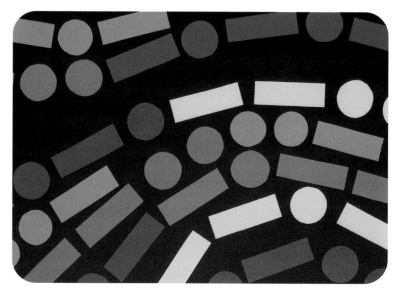

SPEEDY MESSAGES

Morse code sends messages very fast, using sound signals, light flashes or printed dots and dashes. Patterns of dashes and dots, long and short sounds or flashes of light are used. Each pattern stands for one letter of the alphabet. The most famous signal in Morse code is . . . – – – . . . It stands for SOS and is an international signal for emergencies.

LOTS OF LETTERS

Code breakers puzzle out how a code works. Most codes based on scrambling letters are easy to break. In English, some letters are used more than others. You write lots more Es than you do Zs! So, a code breaker starts by counting letters. Soon, they spot the Es and As, and then the other letters. But some codes use a secret key, such as a word or a number that changes with every new message. Did you know that e-mail messages are sent in code? First, a 'public' key scrambles the message so that it cannot be read by anyone else. When it arrives, a secret 'private' key unscrambles it.

A bar code is printed on things we buy. It has 11 bars which stand for the product, the maker, the colour, weight and size. In the shop, a laser scanner decodes each stripe at the checkout.

14

Dial-a-code

WHAT YOU NEED

coloured card

glitter glue

2 plates to draw around

pencil

glue stick

black and silver pens

gold glitter

scissors

paper fastener

darning needle

1 Use plates to help you cut two circles of different sizes from the coloured paper.

2 Make a hole in the centre of each with the needle. Fix together with the paper fastener.

3 Write letters and numbers, evenly spaced, around each circle with the silver and black pens.

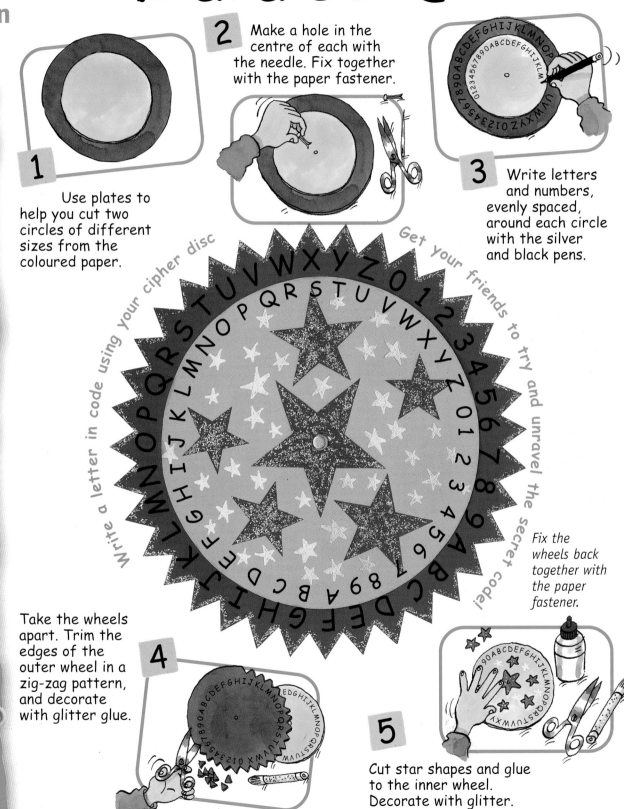

Write a letter in code using your cipher disc

Get your friends to try and unravel the secret code!

Take the wheels apart. Trim the edges of the outer wheel in a zig-zag pattern, and decorate with glitter glue.

4

Fix the wheels back together with the paper fastener.

5 Cut star shapes and glue to the inner wheel. Decorate with glitter.

15

Beautiful books

A hand-made, textured book with cut-out windows and gold-leaf pages.

Some books have pictures in them or stories to tell. Others explain facts or ideas. But books have not always looked as they do now. The first books were just writing carved onto wood or clay tablets.

STORIES ON SCROLLS

About 3,000 years ago, the Chinese made books by writing on long strips of bamboo. In Ancient Egypt, people wrote books on a kind of paper, called papyrus, which was made from the stems of a river plant. Later, the Ancient Greeks and Romans made books out of parchment and vellum, which they made from animal skins.

COPYBOOKS

Until the invention of printing, every book was copied by hand. Medieval monks worked for months to make a book. These had hand-painted pictures and beautiful decorations, and were called illuminated manuscripts. But this way of making books was slow and expensive. Then, in about 1440, the printing press was invented and the first printed books appeared. Today, millions of books are printed all around the world. You can buy them in bookshops or borrow them from a library. They can be hardback or paperback, big or small, in colour or black and white.

Rag book

WHAT YOU NEED

large rectangular piece of black felt

bright and glittery fabric

needle

coloured threads

scissors and pinking shears

wool

sequins

glue

beads

buttons

ribbons

1 Fold the black felt in half lengthwise and then fold into a 'concertina' to create pages. Ask an adult to iron the folds to make them sharp. Flatten out to show 12 pages.

Use a variety of different materials to design other rag books

2 Cut the coloured fabric into various shapes and sizes, and glue onto the felt pages. Sew on beads and buttons and glue on sequins and other trimmings.

3 Fold up the finished book and use buttons and ribbon loops sewn into place for the fasteners.

Make a shooting star bookmark. Cut out 2 star shapes from felt. Sandwich the ends of pieces of ribbon between the stars and glue the stars together. Decorate with beads and sequins.

Spinning discs

Compact discs or CDs are made by burning tiny holes into a chemical spread over a plastic disc. The average music CD can carry 74 minutes of music recorded as 3 billion holes. A strong light beam made by a laser shines on the spinning disc, and the bumps and holes – called pits and lands – are read and changed to sounds. The pits can bend light. That is what makes a rainbow pattern on the surface of the disc.

CD-ROM

Discs contain much more than just music. A CD contains 5 kilometres of recording track, which makes it ideal for recording the long strings of information that computers need. Many programs, including games, can be recorded on a CD. If you can read information on a CD but can't write on it, a CD is called a CD-ROM – Compact Disc–Read Only Memory.

Your great-granny would have wound up a clockwork gramophone to play her favourite tune. Nowadays, discs can hold much more than gramophone records and tapes could. A tape needs to be wound and rewound to find the track you want; but with a disc, you can go to it instantly. No wonder discs are the most popular way of storing music and information. Modern discs can hold hundreds of tunes, and play them back perfectly every time.

MINIDISCS AND MP3

Minidiscs are even smaller than CDs. A minidisc recorder will fit into the palm of your hand. It won't hold much computer data, but it will hold 80 minutes of stereo sound. Pre-recorded minidiscs are like CDs, with pits and lands, but minidiscs you can record on use a layer that can be magnetised when a laser heats it. MP3 players are even smaller. They use special 'flash-memory' chips to record music from the Internet. An MP3 player smaller than a pen can hold two hours of stereo sound.

Musical notes

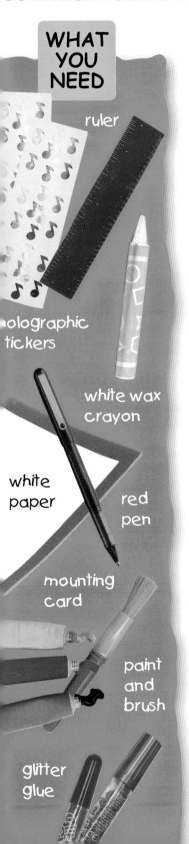

WHAT YOU NEED

ruler

holographic stickers

white wax crayon

white paper

red pen

mounting card

paint and brush

glitter glue

1 Draw large treble and bass clefs in white wax crayon on white paper. Add some big notes.

2 Paint on a yellow and orange wash so that your clefs and notes show through.

3 Use a ruler to draw five-lined staves in red pen.

4 Stick metallic or holographic notes on the lines and in the spaces, so the music travels up and down the staves.

5 Stick on strips of holographic shapes to divide the music into sections.

Use glitter glue to make bar lines. Your melody is complete!

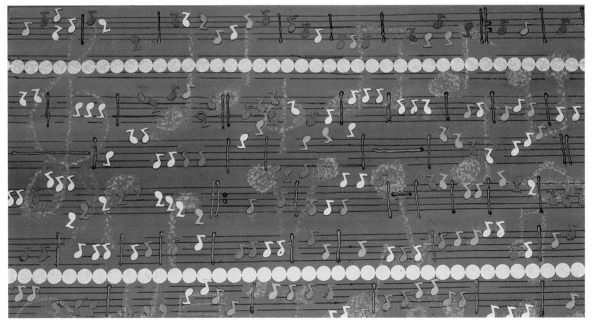

Newsprint

Newspapers print news. They are important because they keep everyone up-to-date with what is going on in the world. As well as letting us know the daily news, they tell interesting stories and pass on useful information.
They let us know the latest score in a football game, and details of TV programmes or films. Some even print cartoons to make us laugh.

LATEST!

The first printed daily newspaper was published in London, 300 years ago. But the idea of written news had been around long before then! In ancient Rome in 59 BC, handwritten sheets of paper were stuck up for people to read. The sheets were called Acta Diurna, which means 'Daily News'. Most modern newspapers are published every day. Sometimes different editions – such as a morning edition, an afternoon edition and an evening edition – are published through the day. Each edition tells the latest news. Some local newspapers only come out once a week. These papers usually just print news about the local area.

HOTTEST!

Reporters collect the news as it happens. Some stories can be sent across the world by phone or the Internet. Photographs are used to go with the best stories. The editor of the newspaper decides which stories will appear in the paper, and especially which will be the top story, printed on the front page.
As well as using eye-catching photographs to attract our attention, strong headlines must also be written! When the newspaper is ready, printing machines print many thousands of copies. The newspapers are folded, packed and sent to shops. All this may happen overnight, so that you can wake up to the latest news in print.

TABLOIDS AND BROADSHEETS

The smaller, tabloid newspapers usually have more sport, gossip about celebrities, and photographs. The larger, broadsheet newspapers usually print news stories in more detail. Both kinds of newspapers have advertisements, which help to pay for the cost of producing the paper.

Newspaper man

WHAT YOU NEED

- small plastic bottle
- 2 hollow plastic balls
- wire
- scissors
- masking tape
- glue
- paste
- cocktail sticks
- small piece of wood or polyboard
- newspapers

Varnish your model with watered-down glue

1 Make two holes in the base of the bottle. Thread through two long pieces of wire, and twist for legs. Cut a ball in half, and push onto legs to form feet.

Make a newspaper from cuttings for your man to hold.

2 Bend two arms with hands and long fingers. Thread each one through holes at the top of the body, and tape to the bottle. Stick model to base.

3 Tape the second ball to the top of the bottle for a head. Coil a strip of paper around part of a cocktail stick and jab it into the ball for the nose.

4 Paste strips of newspaper all over the model. Cut individual letters from newsprint to make eyes and mouth. Cover base with colourful newspaper photos.

Stamps and postmarks

It's exciting to get a letter through the post, especially if it has travelled a long way across the world! You can tell if a letter has come from abroad by looking at the stamp. Every country in the world creates its own set of stamps.

THE PENNY BLACK

When we post a letter or parcel, we buy postage stamps to stick on the outside. These pay for the cost of delivering it. The first postage stamp was used in Britain in 1840. It had a picture of Queen Victoria on it, and it was named the Penny Black.

FROM RUNNER TO AIRMAIL

At first, letters were carried by people on foot or taken by horse, stagecoach or ship. A letter might take months to arrive! Later, letters and parcels were delivered on special trains, and aeroplanes carried airmail to faraway countries. Today, about a billion items go by post across the world every day. They are collected, sorted and delivered, often overnight. Delivery is made quicker by postcodes that tell the post person where to deliver them. Some of these can be recognised by sorting machines. The stamp is 'franked' with a postmark. This tells you where the letter was posted and when.

A collection of stamps from around the world.

Design-a-stamp

WHAT YOU NEED

strong white paper

pencil

ruler

paintbrush

glue stick

paints

used stamps

black paper

scissors and pinking shears

1 Choose a theme for your stamps, eg: famous artists.

2 Draw a narrow border around the edge of the paper. In pencil, draw your designs within the border. Paint in bright colours.

3 To make a collage stamp, sort used stamps into colour groups and glue them in an interesting design.

4 Draw the profile of a friend on black paper. Cut out and stick in the corner of each stamp.

Design envelopes and note paper to go with your stamps

5 Finish by cutting around each stamp with pinking shears.

Mount your stamps on coloured card to make a display for your bedroom wall.

23

Body language

Did you know that you can show your thoughts and feelings without speaking? You do this with your body language. Smiles and frowns are body language. So is the way you sit or stand. How you look or move sends out messages about how you are feeling.

EYES DOWN

It is easy to talk to someone who looks at you and nods. This means they are listening. But a person who crosses their arms and looks away is sending a signal to say they are not listening. Some people may look down when they are being told off. This means they are sorry.

MIND YOUR FEET!

People from different places and cultures use body language in different ways. In some countries it is rude to show the sole of your foot to someone. So be careful how you sit! Making a 'thumbs up' sign means 'good' in Europe and North America. But in the Middle East, it is very rude!

PLAYING TO THE CROWD

You can tell a whole story without words, through movement. This is called mime. Mime artists can make us imagine other people and things around them by the way they move. In a similar way, when a dancer moves to music, the audience can tell what is happening and how the dancer is feeling.

SIGN LANGUAGE

Languages for people with hearing difficulties combine mouthing the words and making hand and arm movements. Lip-reading and following the movements can make understanding as easy as listening.

Mime artists wear face paints to exaggerate facial expressions, and add drama to performances.

Theatrical masks

WHAT YOU NEED

gold and silver card

pencil

scissors

glue

sequins

glitter

glass or plastic gems

darning needle

elastic

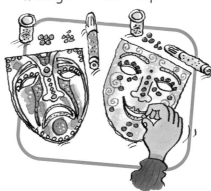

1 Cut out mask outlines from silver and gold card. Now cut out happy (comic) features from one, and sad (tragic) from the other.

2 Draw patterns on the shiny side of each mask, then decorate with glitter and sequins.

3 Make a hole by the side of each eye with a darning needle. Thread elastic through the holes and knot behind the mask. You could also make hand-held masks by glueing them to sticks.

Decorate your tragedy mask in cold colours with bold patterns and shadows

Decorate your comedy mask in warm colours and swirly glitter patterns

Television

When you look at a television screen, your eyes are fooled. What you think is a colour picture is just a mixture of red, green and blue dots! And when the pictures change quickly, you think they are moving. In fact, the pictures on the screen are still, and it is only because the dots, or pixels, change so fast, that you see a moving image.

THE CAMERA END

A television camera splits the light from a scene into red, green and blue. The colours are then changed into a code of tiny electric signals, and linked with coded sound signals. Then both picture and sound are broadcast – or sent out – through the air as radio waves.

THE TELEVISION END

A television set is like a box with three colour guns at one end and a glass screen at the other. The screen is coated inside with a special chemical called phosphor. When the guns fire tiny electric signals at the screen, the phosphor gives out dots of red, green or blue light, and the picture appears.

BRINGING YOUR PICTURE

Not all of the pictures you see on television are broadcast from a studio. You may be seeing images that have been 'bounced' across the world from a geostationary satellite. This is a satellite that is fixed in space at the right height to turn with the Earth. Or you may be watching a programme that has travelled under the ground through a cable.

Goggle-box

WHAT YOU NEED

shoe box and lid

bottle lids

tracing paper

glue

tin foil

thread

paint and brush

scissors

silver pen

tinsel

black and white paper

acetate

pipe cleaners

1 Cut a rectangular hole in both the underside of the box and the lid, for the TV screen and the light source. Paint both in a bright colour.

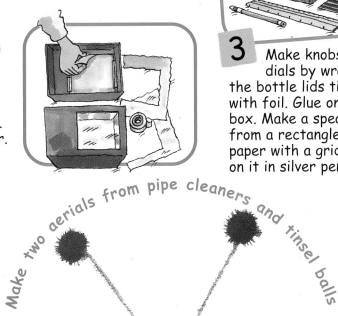

2 Cut out an acetate screen, and use a sheet of tracing paper, for the back of the TV. Glue in place behind the cut-out holes.

3 Make knobs and dials by wrapping the bottle lids tightly with foil. Glue onto the box. Make a speaker from a rectangle of black paper with a grid drawn on it in silver pen.

4 Draw a scene onto pape. Colour and cut out the elements of the picture separately. Take the lid off the box and hang each part of the picture by 2 threads. Glue inside the TV, at different distances from the screen to create a clever 3D effect.

Make two aerials from pipe cleaners and tinsel balls

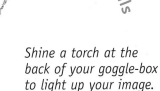

Shine a torch at the back of your goggle-box to light up your image.

27

Computerland

Can you really believe what you see? When you watch a film or a television programme, you might be seeing a world entirely created on a computer. Recent films have starred computer-generated actors, or placed real actors in virtual worlds – from dinosaur habitats to the Colosseum in Rome. Computer games create imaginary worlds that you can interact with, and Virtual Reality goes one step further, by placing you in cyberspace.

DIGITAL DOTS

Pictures can be drawn as dots on the screen and every dot given a number. This is called digitising. Once you have digitised pictures – or sounds – you can change them any way you like, and make almost anything happen. The computer graphic you make is called a bitmap.

COMPUTER GAMES

When you play a computer game, you are watching a bitmap. The bitmap is changing so fast that you are carried along by the game. By moving and clicking a mouse or moving a joystick, you can change the bitmap.

VIRTUAL REALITY

Using today's computer technology, you can enter a world that is almost real. VR, or Virtual Reality, takes you into cyberspace – an imaginary world. VR goggles project a 3-D picture of cyberspace for you, and stereo headphones add the sound. A special glove records every movement of your hand, so that you can interact with this virtual world. Lift your arm and VR technology responds – you can even turn round and pick things up. Whole-body VR suits can make cyberspace even more realistic

With these virtual reality goggles, you can escape into a computer-generated world.

Crazy computer

WHAT YOU NEED

- cardboard boxes and tube
- silver and red foil
- plastic bottle lids
- sequins
- metallic card
- wire
- 2 corks
- small plastic food containers
- tape
- scissors
- silver and black card
- glue
- white paper
- metal paper mesh

1 Wrap 4 boxes in silver foil. Seal the ends with glue or tape.

2 Coil wire by wrapping around the tube. Glue on sequins and push ends of wire into the corks. Glue onto the biggest box for antennae.

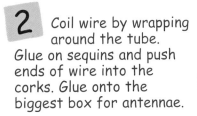

3 Glue black shapes and a sequin in the centre of two white lids for the film reels. Glue onto the front of the big box.

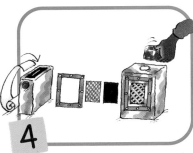

4 Make a printer and a power unit from the small boxes. Decorate with foil knobs, metallic card frames, mesh and sequin 'screws'.

Make a glitzy control panel! Wrap foil around bottle lids for knobs. Make dials from plastic pot lids, paper and sequins.

Make flashing red lights from foil-covered bottle tops

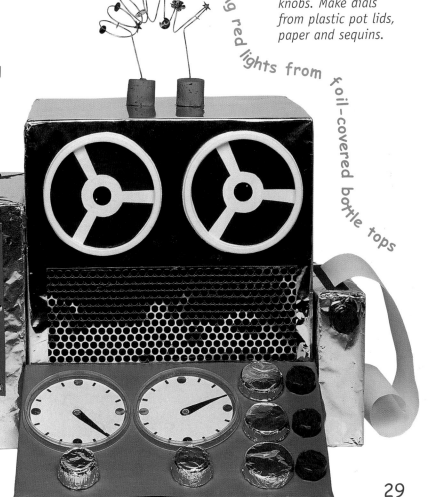

Wired up

Telephones turn sounds into electrical signals, and these signals are carried on copper wires from your home to the telephone exchange. Here the signals are sent through optical fibres – long strands of glass – to the person you are calling. Their telephone turns the message back to sound. On the way, the message may travel across the country or under the sea – or it may be bounced from a satellite in space.

MAKING CONNECTIONS

When there were very few telephones, you could call a person, the operator, and tell them who you wanted to speak to. They would pull and push plugs at the telephone exchange and put your call through. Now, with millions of calls every minute, they are handled automatically.

HANDY MOBILES

You don't need to stand still to make a phone call. Mobile phones send a signal that is picked up by a base station. Most countries have been divided into areas called 'cells', and each cell has a base station. Wherever you happen to be calling from, you are in one of these cells, and so a base station is nearby. The base station puts your call on the telephone network, and your friend, standing in another cell near a base station far away, hears your signal sent to their mobile phone.

PICTURES BY PHONE

Telephone lines don't just carry voices. They can carry documents, sent by a facsimile machine, or fax, that changes an image to a code. The fax machine scans the document, then it sends it to another fax that prints it out in words and pictures. Telephone lines can also carry messages between computers – in pictures, words and sounds.

Funky phones

WHAT YOU NEED

2 yogurt pots

fake fur fabric

pen

scraps of coloured felt

beads and sequins

feather trim

darning needle

scissors or pinking shears

strong glue

thick string or wool

1 Cut two rectangles of fur fabric long enough to wrap around each pot and glue in place.

2 Draw around the bottom of a pot and cut 2 circles of black felt with pinking shears. Glue onto pot bases.

3 Cut noses from pink felt and make the eyes using circles of black and white felt with sequins and beads.

4 Glue semi-circles of black and pink felt together for the ears. Fold the sides in as shown and glue the ears to the rims of the pots.

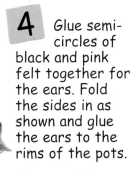

Use your phone to talk to a friend

To use your phone, face a friend and pull the string tight between you. Hold a pot to your ear while your friend talks clearly into the other one. Their voice will pass along the string as vibrations.

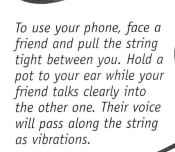

5 Make hair by cutting the feather trim in half. Pierce the base of each pot with the darning needle. Thread the string through both pots and knot on the inside.

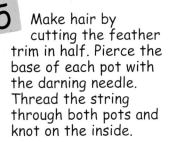

31

On the Web

*A*ll over the world, millions of computers in homes, schools and offices are connected to the Internet. The Internet allows people to explore the World Wide Web, which we shorten to www, and to keep in contact with each other by e-mail.

GLOBAL NETWORK

The Internet is an international network of computers, which talk to each other by cable, telephone and radio. It began in the USA in 1969, as a Department of Defence computer network called ARPANET. Researchers in other areas then began to use it, along with a similar program called NSF. By the mid 1990s, the Internet was available to everyone with a computer.

GIANT ENCYCLOPEDIA

The World Wide Web is part of the Internet. It is like a giant encyclopedia, containing text, pictures, sound and video. If you need information in a hurry, the Web is often the best place to look. The Web was invented in 1992 by Tim Berners-Lee. He invented a code called Hypertext Markup Language, or HTML. This allows items in separate documents – or even on different computers – to be linked.

SURFING THE NET

You can explore the Web or 'surf the net', using a computer program called a 'browser'. Then you can use a 'search engine' to look for information on any subject that interests you. Or you can hop from one subject to another – just for fun!

Weave a web

Create a unique and personal web site

WHAT YOU NEED

- feathers
- string
- bamboo canes
- gold or silver spray paint
- beads and sequins
- scissors
- ribbon
- strong glue

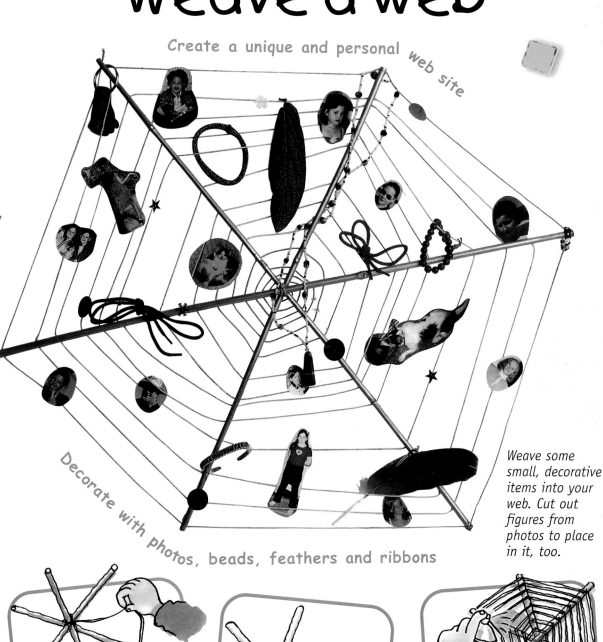

Decorate with photos, beads, feathers and ribbons

Weave some small, decorative items into your web. Cut out figures from photos to place in it, too.

1 Place three pieces of bamboo in a star shape and tie them together in the middle with string.

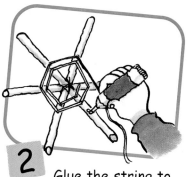

2 Glue the string to the middle of the star and wind it out in a spiral, sticking it to the bamboo as you go.

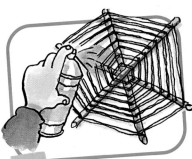

3 When the web is complete, spray it gold or silver. Ask an adult to help you.

33

Satellite signals

A photograph of Earth at night taken by a satellite.

Today, there are many hundreds of satellites whirling around the Earth, doing important work for people on the ground. Satellites have an amazing view of the world below.

ARTIFICIAL SATELLITES

A satellite is a machine designed to travel in space. It goes round, or orbits, Earth. Each satellite has a small motor to keep it at the correct height and in the correct orbit. A ground control centre tracks the satellite and sends it orders.

SPY AND SCIENTIFIC SATELLITES

Spy satellites are used by governments and military forces. They check the weapons, armies and military bases of other countries. Scientific satellites do a wide range of work. For example, the Landsat satellite studies Earth, showing where oil and minerals might be found.

COMMUNICATIONS SATELLITES

We use this kind of satellite every day without knowing it! Satellites such as Comstar and Intelsat send television signals round the world. They also send millions of telephone calls, many of which contain information being sent on the Internet.

Silver satellite

WHAT YOU NEED

2 boxes

2 foil pie cases

scissors

foil

holographic paper

2 wooden sticks

silver paper

tape

strong glue

glittery pipe cleaners

'pull-up' bottle tops from water bottles

1 Cover the large box with foil and the smaller one with silver paper. Decorate both with squares, triangles and stripes of holographic paper, and stick the boxes together.

Make a small dish and a radar on glittery pipe cleaners.

2 Pierce a hole in each end of the main box to hold a wooden stick.

3 Cut a section from one of the pie dishes as shown, and glue to form a cone shape for the large 'dish'. Push over the end of the stick and tape in place. Use bottle tops for decoration.

Decorate bottle tops, and attach to your box to make boosters!

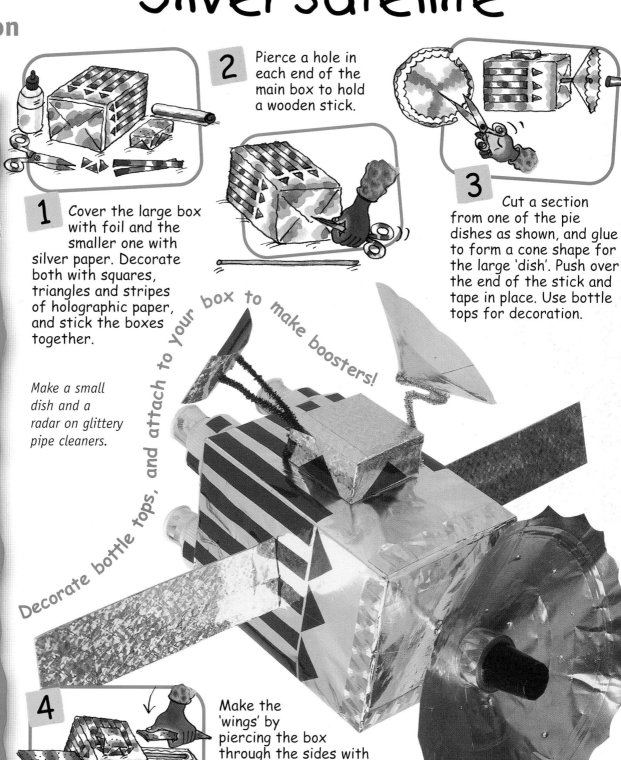

4 Make the 'wings' by piercing the box through the sides with another stick. Glue holographic strips over both sides of the stick to form rotating panels.

35

Microchips

CHIPS AND PCs

The invention of the microchip made small personal computers, or PCs, possible. Huge memories and calculating power could be put into a tiny box. Modern computers can do a billion different things every second. The Central Processing Unit, or CPU, contains so many fast-working chips that it gets hot and may need a fan to cool it down.

RAM AND ROM

Computers have two sorts of memory. RAM is Random Access Memory. RAM chips are used to store the programs and data you are working on. They change the picture as you play a computer game. ROM, or Read Only Memory, chips may store the game itself – the instructions and rules. Computer games are usually on a CD-ROM or a DVD-ROM, which you put into your computer before you play.

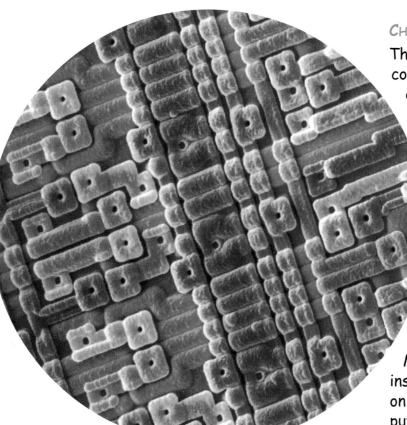

The magnified surfaces of a silicon chip (above) and a microprocessor chip (right).

The first computers were so big, you could walk around inside them. Then, in 1959, tiny patches of a chemical called silicon, linked by metal tracks, were used to take the place of the biggest parts. In 1971, the first computer 'chip' was made, putting all the memory and calculating power onto a tiny scrap of silicon. This first chip had 2,300 patches of silicon on it; by 1999, the average chip had 10 million.

COMPUTER MICE

When you use a computer, your mouse changes your hand movements into electrical signals. Operating the mouse moves a cursor, or pointer, on the screen. Pressing a button on the mouse sends your instruction to the computer.

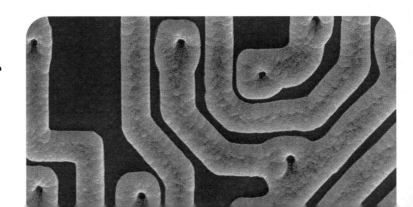

Circuit board

WHAT YOU NEED

large sheet of green paper

scissors

coloured paper

glue

small plastic tubes

large piece of corrugated card

1mm wire

assorted boxes and cartons

pencil

1 Make a base board by glueing green paper to the corrugated card.

2 Arrange the boxes and plastic tubes on the board. These will be the microchips and resistors. Draw around them for 'positionals'.

4 Cover the microchip boxes in coloured paper, decorate and glue in position.

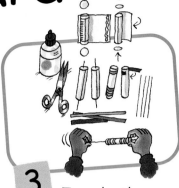

3 To make the resistors, cover the tubes and decorate with strips of coloured paper of various widths. Ask an adult to make holes in the base board. Attach wire to the resistors, then thread it through the holes, and glue underneath to secure.

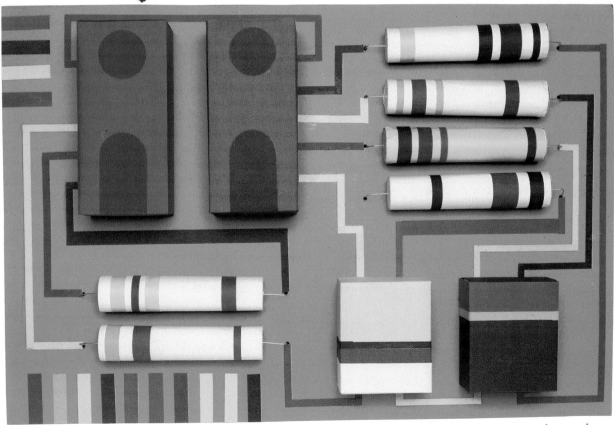

Cut strips of coloured paper to connect all the components on your board

Amazing adverts

Advertisements are everywhere. We see them on TV, at the cinema, on the Internet, in magazines and in the street. They are there to grab our attention, to change the way we think – and to make us buy something! The bigger and brighter they are, the more likely they are to make an impact and catch our eye.

FACE THE FACTS

An advertisement tells you important facts about something. It might be a breakfast cereal or the latest computer game. You usually see a picture of the goods, and its special features are pointed out in a catchy phrase called a slogan. The slogan might say that something is tasty, healthy, long-lasting or even good-looking! The idea is to make something sound so good that people will want to buy it.

HIDDEN MEANINGS

Many modern adverts contain hidden messages – we don't always know what they are about. You have to look carefully to find out what the company is advertising. If a television advert makes you watch and wonder, you are more likely to remember it.

BRAND NAMES

The shapes, colours and words of different brands of goods are carefully protected from being copied. A popular brand name is very valuable. A soft-drink brand may be worth billions of dollars. Manufacturers of sports clothes make their brand badges or logos so famous that words aren't needed on trainers and caps. Brand thieves, called pirates, try to copy products, such as music, computer games and clothing. This is illegal and manufacturers spend millions of dollars protecting their brands.

A street in Tokyo lit up by hundreds of advertising signs.

Magnetic billboard

WHAT YOU NEED

ite card

black pen

glue

coloured pencils

scissors

foil

tinsel

small magnets

baking tray

ribbon or gold thread

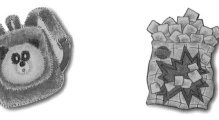

1

Draw a variety of food adverts with whacky background shapes, and colour them in.

Make up some of your own brand logos and slogans

2

Cut around each advert and glue a magnet to the back.

3

Make a magnet board from the baking tray. Place it face down and glue a sheet of foil to the surface. Glue tinsel to the edges to decorate.

4

Attach a piece of ribbon or gold thread to the back of the tray to hang it up. Arrange your magnet adverts on the board.

39

Keypads and gadgets

Nowadays, wherever you are you can phone home, play a computer game or write a text message. These are all possible because gadgets are getting smaller and smaller. They are halving in size every few months – but also becoming more powerful.

POCKET PALS

The palm top computer is small enough to fit into your pocket but is hugely powerful. You can use it to keep your diary: an infra-red beam can send your message to another palm top, and it can even read your handwriting! You can also carry a miniature television in your pocket. The latest models have a tiny screen that mixes red, blue and green light to create the picture.

THROW–AWAY PHONES

Mobile phones are getting smaller, too. The first ones were as big as a brick, but today's models are the size of a small chocolate bar. As well as telephone calls and text messages, they can receive faxes or access the Internet. All this is possible because the information is digitised – made into a string of instructions. The same 'string' can carry two or more messages. This system is called multiplexing, and it allows you to access the Internet while making a telephone call. An American company has recently developed a disposable mobile phone. It is made of a special paper, and instead of wires it uses ink that conducts electricity. You buy it, use it and then throw it away! Wristwatch telephones are also being developed. Many companies already use wristwatch beepers so they can keep in touch with their workers when they are out and about.

Large keyboards are mainly used in offices and homes. When people are travelling around they take the smaller pocket-sized keypad gadgets.

Screen saver picture

old magazines

pencils

scissors

glue stick

squared paper

tracing paper

ruler

1 Choose a simple subject for your collage from a photo or picture with lots of colour contrast. Copy the picture onto graph paper, using tracing paper if necessary.

2 Find pictures in magazines with the colours you need. Draw a square grid, and cut along the lines to makes 1cm squares.

3 Work on one area at a time. Glue the square pieces onto your picture using shades of your chosen colour. As you go along, stand back from your collage to make sure you can see the picture clearly.

Add shiny paper squares for a dazzling effect

41

Animatronics

A scene from the computer-animated film Antz. *Models were made of each of the characters, which were then scanned and made into computer images.*

REMOTE CONTROL

Animatronic creations are often used for close-up shots in films or for scenes where a remote-controlled model has to do something in a particular situation – whether it is eating grass or swimming in the sea. These can be linked with computer-generated scenes to make the creature come to life.

COMPUTERISED IMAGES

Computer-generated imagery, or CGI, makes it possible to make films without using live actors at all. A dinosaur model, scanned by laser and changed by a computer into thousands of tiny parts, can be moved into life-like positions on screen. An artist takes great care to make the dinosaur look as realistic as possible so the that creature comes to life. Actors can also be combined with CGI. For instance, actors dressed as gladiators can battle in a scene from Ancient Rome that only exists on computer.

Animatronics is a way of making models move realistically. A complicated network of wires carry electronic messages to electric motors that make eyes swivel, arms move and fingers grip. Animatronic models or robots can make museum visits exciting or add to the fun at theme parks.

STOP-ACTION

Flexible models can be made and then filmed, frame by frame (picture by picture), to look as though they are moving. A plasticine model has to be moved 25 times to make one second of animated film. A full-length animated film consists of thousands of still frames of the models or drawings, which together create a moving picture.

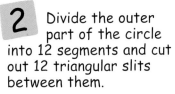

Stroboscope!

WHAT YOU NEED

black thin card

white card

glitter glues

scissors

sequins

felt pens

cork

tracing paper

dinner plate

sewing pin

chunky pad

pencil

black pen

two small beads

1 Draw around a plate and cut out a circle from the white card. Using a compass, draw a small circle inside the big circle.

2 Divide the outer part of the circle into 12 segments and cut out 12 triangular slits between them.

3 In the spaces left, draw 12 identical boxes, using tracing paper to reproduce them. Add a clown popping out of the box, showing more of his face each time. Draw a spiral in the middle of the disc. Colour in.

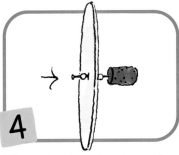

4 Thread a bead onto a pin, and poke it through the centre of the disc. Put another bead on the other side, and secure with a cork for a smooth spin.

Flipbook

1. Draw a stick figure to be the 'star' of your book. Plan a sequence of 10 action pictures against a simple background.
2. Draw the first frame on page one. Turn over and repeat the frame, making small changes to the figure's actions.
3. When you get to the end of the sequence, remove any leftover blank pages.
4. Make a book cover using black card, glitter glue and sequins.

Animal chat

Have you ever seen two dogs saying hello? They sniff each other and sometimes wag their tails. But if one dog feels threatened, it will put back its ears and even growl. It is telling the other dog to watch out! Although animals do not actually speak to each other, they can communicate in all kinds of ways.

SIGN LANGUAGE

Humans use their faces to signal their feelings, and our nearest relatives, chimpanzees, also use their facial expressions to communicate. Humans have even been able to train chimpanzees to learn sign language. One chimp called Washoe learned to use 150 signs, and to understand 300. Honeybees are insects that use a sign language. Special dances show the direction, distance and size of nectar and pollen stores.

IN TOUCH

Elephants keep in touch with each other by making deep sounds. Howler monkeys scream at one another among the treetops. But animals also send messages with scents. A dog lifting its leg at every lamp post is marking its territory. The feathery antennae of a male moth can pick up the scent of a female moth a long way away.

WHALE NOISE

Whales and dolphins are very intelligent animals who communicate by making sounds. Some whales sing songs to attract a mate. They make chirps, screams, whistles, clicks and grunts! Dolphins are so clever that we have even been able to teach some to speak a few words.

Ocarina turtles

WHAT YOU NEED

large smooth pebble

air-drying clay

clear food wrap

stick

table knife

black felt-tip pen

1 Wrap the pebble in food wrap. Roll a ball of clay larger than the pebble, and push your thumb into the middle. Place the pebble into the hole and push the clay over the end to seal. Roll to make a smooth surface.

2 Allow the pebble to partly dry overnight. Cut a line around the middle of the pebble with the knife. Make holes in the top with the stick and another in the end for the mouthpiece.

3 Pull the two halves apart and remove the pebble and food wrap. Stick the turtle back together with wet clay.

4 Make head and legs from small balls of clay. Stick another ball over the mouthpiece and open with a flat stick.

5 Leave to dry for 2 days, then decorate with black felt-tip pen.

Blow into the mouthpiece, covering the holes with your fingers

45

Glossary and Index